THEOSOPHY

THE WISDOM OF THE AGES

Cherry Gilchrist

HarperSanFrancisco
An Imprint of HarperCollins*Publishers*

A LABYRINTH BOOK

THEOSOPHY: THE WISDOM OF THE AGES

Printed in Hong Kong

For information address
HarperCollins*Publishers*, 10 East 53rd Street, New York, NY 10022.

HarperCollins ®, 🏭 ®, and HarperSanFrancisco™ are trademarks of HarperCollins Publishers Inc.

HarperCollins Web Site: http: //www. harpercollins. com

1

FIRST EDITION

THEOSOPHY was produced by Labyrinth Publishing (UK) Ltd
Design by DW Design
Typesetting by DW Design in London, England

Library of Congress Cataloging-in-Publication Data

Gilchrist, Cherry.
    Theosophy: the wisdom of the ages/Cherry Gilchrist. – – 1st ed.
    p. cm.
Includes bibliographical references.
ISBN 0–06–251306–0 (alk. paper)
1. Theosophy. I. Title.
BP565. G5T47 1996   95–33028
299'. 934 – – dc20   CIP

96 97 98 99 00 LAB 10 9 8 7 6 5 4 3 2 1

CONTENTS

INTRODUCTION 1

THE BIRTH OF THEOSOPHY 7

CYCLES OF CREATION 17

HUMAN DESTINY 25

THE HIDDEN MASTERS 31

SUBTLE BODIES 43

THEOSOPHY TODAY 51

BIBLIOGRAPHY 60

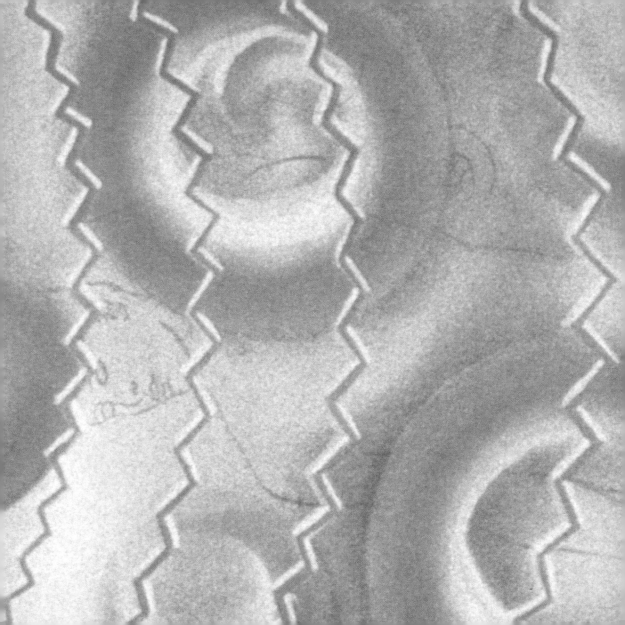

INTRODUCTION

Frontispiece: The Heart Chakra, from C.W. Leadbeater. Subtle forms of energy can be detected and described. Here the qualities of "heart energy" are shown through color and pattern.

Previous page: Devotion, from A. Besant and C.W. Leadbeater.

Wisdom takes many forms. It is the source from which fertile inspiration comes, and it arises beyond the framework of time and space in which our human lives are enmeshed. It is close to the creative energy of the universe itself, and as such cannot be restricted or tied to any one set of ideas, beliefs or instructions, though each of those sets may contain a drop of wisdom which has given them life. As seekers after wisdom, we need to be both active in our search, and receptive to the flow of wisdom. We cannot manufacture it, yet we have to be responsive to it, and to work in developing the knowledge that it brings.

Those who are prepared to serve wisdom often come up against the fixed views of the day and are branded as rebels or heretics. Wisdom does not necessarily support the existing status quo, and it may also contain the seeds of the future within it, which is anathema to people and organizations who fear change. Throughout history, seekers after wisdom have had to face challenges from "the establishment" of the day. Sufis, Kabbalists, and Gnostics have been rejected many times by orthodox religion. Groups such as the Cathars suffered total extermination for their ideas, and individuals such as John Dee,

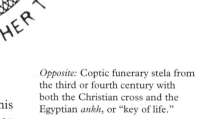

William Blake, and Pico della Mirandola all struck out alone to follow their own paths of revelation.

Theosophy embodies a search for wisdom which had to struggle against the closed religious views of the nineteenth and early twentieth centuries. Other occult and esoteric lines of the time were forging their own paths quietly, but whereas they tended to pursue one distinct line of enquiry, Theosophy aimed to fling open the gates to reveal the splendor of universal wisdom, a wisdom buried at the heart of all genuine religious and occult traditions. Out of this broad perspective, a new vision was born, for a new context had to be created to contain and to re-formulate this wisdom. Theosophy has helped to open the human mind to universal truths, and to set up a new framework through which they could be understood.

At our present point in time, we can recognize just how necessary it is to extend our vision. The Earth is beginning to seem very small—but out there are stars and space, the great unknown.

Opposite: Coptic funerary stela from the third or fourth century with both the Christian cross and the Egyptian *ankh,* or "key of life."

Above: The logo of the Theosophical Society combines different symbols: the Egyptian ankh is surrounded by two interlocking pyramids, representing the union of heaven and earth, and encircled by the alchemical serpent, the *ouroboros.*

3

People fight to the death over minor divisions of religious belief—but where is the sense in that? Isn't the truth that links them more important? Theosophy shows that these limited views have their own reality, but only as a part of the greater cycles of creation. And it also teaches that we, as human beings, can gain access to this exalted and expanded universe and experience the wisdom of its workings for ourselves. Though its origins lie in the nineteenth century, the theosophical perspective has much in common with that of the New Age, and, it can fairly be said, it is the impetus of Theosophy that has enabled the whole New Age movement to come into being.

Opposite: Starry Night over the Rhone, by Vincent van Gogh (1853–90). Here the artist intuitively expresses the infinity of space, embodying the extended view of creation taught by Theosophy.

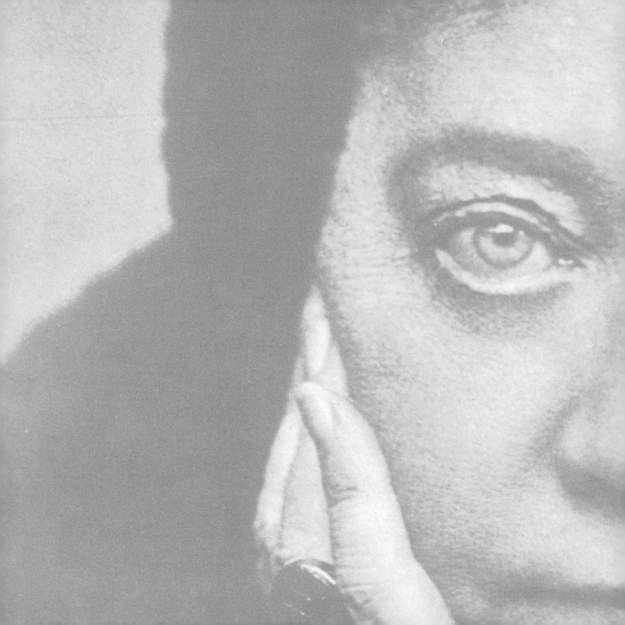

THE BIRTH OF THEOSOPHY

A Meeting with a Crocodile

Previous page: Madame Helena Petrovna Blavatsky (1831–91). A famous portrait of the renowned founder of the Theosophical Society, remarked on by many people who met her as a powerful and magnetic figure. Born in the Ukraine, she has been commemorated in her home town.

Above: Helena Blavatsky and Henry Steel Olcott. Colonel Olcott was an indefatigable helper of Blavatsky who played an important part in the establishment of the Theosophical Society in New York in 1875.

In the winter of 1888, a newspaper reporter entered a house in Holland Park, London, with some trepidation. The woman he had come to interview, he had been told, was as tough as "a sacred crocodile of the old Nile." Ushered into her sitting room, his fears were not at first allayed; his eyes met a powerful gaze, in a heavy, almost swarthy face. Was she, he wondered, a kind of female magician? He had heard tales about the mysterious psychic phenomena that often happened in her presence. The parlor was atmospheric, wreathed in smoke, with lamps glowing like a "triple star." She did not get up to meet him; her heavy body, swathed in black silk, was by now almost entirely incapacitated. Instead, chain-smoking, she began a fascinating conversation which held him spellbound for several hours.

She told him that there is a truth that underlies all religions, but that one must search for it under their external forms and ceremonies. She spoke about the higher faculties of man, and how these can be developed, and gave him the encouragement that the path of wisdom lies open to the genuine seeker.

This was Madame Helena Petrovna Blavatsky, one of the most colorful characters in esoteric history. Born in 1831 in the Ukraine, she was by this time a much-traveled, multi-lingual philosopher and teacher and prime founder of the Theosophical Society as it still exists today. Our anonymous reporter was not disappointed with his interview, commenting that she was "a lady of exceptional charm … wonderful variety of information, and powers of conversation which recall the giant talkers of a bygone literary age." All that he missed was a display of any psychic phenomena, which Madame Blavatsky emphatically refused to put on for him. Her abilities as a medium were already the subject of much controversy, and she was keen to avoid further charges of sensationalism.

A portrait on the wall caught the reporter's attention; it showed "a dark and beautiful Indian face, full of sweetness and wisdom." He learned that this was the Mahatma Morya, one of the Masters who instructed "HPB," as she was affectionately known to her followers. The Masters are adepts living on higher planes, who are said to be responsible for the transmission of many of the theosophical teachings, as we shall see later.

An accomplished linguist, Madame Blavatsky moved confidently through the world, absorbing and disseminating mystical teaching from Russia to Egypt, India, Europe and America.

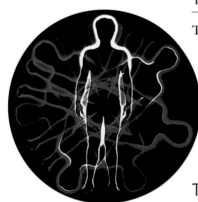

The Seven Levels of Man, by Sid Murray-Clark. A modern representation of the seven subtle bodies said to make up the complete human being. The circular form is an interesting variant on the more usual "layered" version of multiple bodies.

THEOSOPHY DEFINED

The word "theosophy" comes from the Greek, and means "wisdom of God," and "of things divine." The term was used by early Neo-Platonists in Alexandria, and subsequently by followers of the great seventeenth-century alchemical-Christian mystic Jakob Boehme, who, later in the eighteenth century, called one of their study groups The London Theosophical Society. But the term Theosophy, as used in this book, applies to that body of teachings initiated by Madame Blavatsky, and expounded by the Theosophical Society as we know it today.

THE THEOSOPHICAL MESSAGE

The essential message of these teachings is that the scale of existence is a vast, but not uncharted realm; there is a Divine Plan, which manifests itself through various planes of reality, of which the physical world is the lowest. Every person already partakes of these planes of existence, even though he or she may normally be unaware of it. And we each have possibilities for knowledge, wisdom and self-development; we can learn to attune our beings more finely to these different levels of consciousness. It is not a static picture, for everything moves in greater or lesser cycles of creation. Both mankind as a whole and each individual soul is evolving, working its way through numerous incarnations, on the cycle of return to God.

Blavatsky's own search began by asking certain fundamental questions: "When, years ago, we first traveled over the East..., two saddening and ever-occurring questions oppressed our thoughts: WHERE, WHO, WHAT IS GOD? Who ever saw the IMMORTAL SPIRIT of man, so as to be able to assure himself of man's immortality?"

When she came into contact with certain wise men of the East, she discovered that their timeless knowledge could banish such despair. "They showed us that by combining science with religion, the existence of God and immortality of man's spirit may be demonstrated like a problem of Euclid." It was not long before she gathered followers around her, who found illumination in her vision of a purposeful universe which transcends the limitations of religious doctrines, and in which every soul has its part to play.

Thought forms of people from two different schools of teaching. *Above left:* A theosophist's intellectual conception of cosmic order. The upward-pointing triangle signifies the threefold aspect of the spirit, while the interlacing downward-pointing triangle indicates the three inherent qualities of matter.
Above: A perception of the Logos in man, possibly by a Freemason. The five-pointed star has long been the symbol of God manifest in man. The pale blue reflects the devotional feeling of the thinker.

THE NINETEENTH-CENTURY VIEW

If we can think ourselves back to nine-teenth-century Europe and America, the limitations on vision that existed become very apparent, for materialistic science was gaining the upper hand, and Christianity was in a straight-jacketed phase where believers were not expected to think for themselves, or try to find their own way into the sacred mysteries. Spiritually speaking, Western civilization was gasping for fresh air. Today, we take for granted our access to esoteric and religious studies of all kinds, but this openness owes a lot to the advent of Theosophy. Blavatsky burst like a primal force onto the European scene, and though her teachings came like a howling winter wind to the orthodox, to those eager for new horizons, they blew open a door to other worlds.

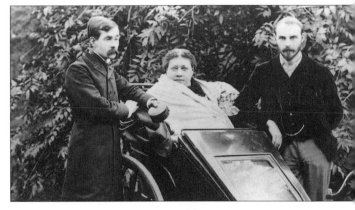

Opposite: Where are we? Who are we? Where are we going? by Paul Gauguin, 1897. The urge to escape the conventions of nineteenth-century European society was intense for those who sought the answers to these questions. Gauguin found inspiration in the vibrant and colorful lives of "primitive" people, while Theosophy sought them from within the great teachings of the world.

Above: Theosophy influenced many men and women of note; on the right of Madame Blavatsky is G.R.S. Mead, an accomplished author and translator of Gnostic teachings.

Above: Isis Unveiled, published in 1877.

Opposite: Annie Besant (1847–1933), one of the most notable "second generation" theosophists, famous for her research into astral and psychic aspects of human experience.

The Life of Blavatsky

Even her critics (and there were many) did not deny that she was a formidable woman. She was born into an aristocratic family as Helena von Hahn, and as a young girl married a widower named Nikifor Blavatsky. Although she left him soon afterwards, she retained his name throughout her life. There was a long-standing interest in occultism and freemasonry in her family, and she had access to books on the subject from an early age. The next step in her quest was to travel to Eastern Europe and Egypt, where she founded an occult society in 1872. She went on to journey in India and the East, and claimed to have spent time learning from the Masters in Tibet.

Her writings, of which the most famous are *Isis Unveiled* and *The Secret Doctrine*, are extraordinary mines of information on inner traditions East and West. She used these as fuel for her grand vision, in which she set forth a synthesis of what she considered to be the most fundamental and essential truths of these teachings. Although they are in one sense global, they have a strong Buddhist and Indian leaning, and Theosophy itself became an important vehicle for bringing Eastern teachings to the West. As her reputation grew, she gathered disciples around her, and out of this the Theosophical Society was born in New York in 1875. Her last years included a period in which she worked intensively on *The Secret Doctrine*, living at various residences in Europe, increasingly crippled with gout and rheumatism. The Countess Constance Wachtmeister, who became one of her most devoted attendants, related how Blavatsky rarely left the house, often working at her desk from six in the morning till seven in the evening without a break. Her energy was remarkable, and even when pronounced at death's door by her doctors she rallied once more, relating how her Master had visited her and offered her a choice between dying, as relief for her suffering, and the chance to finish her work on Earth.

She died in 1891, leaving behind her a Society which has since proved fertile ground for those searching for inner wisdom. Her framework of teachings has been filled out and developed further by her followers, most notably by Annie Besant and C.W. Leadbeater. However, most Theosophists regard Blavatsky's own writings as the supreme source for their philosophy, and no one has yet superseded her contribution to Theosophy.

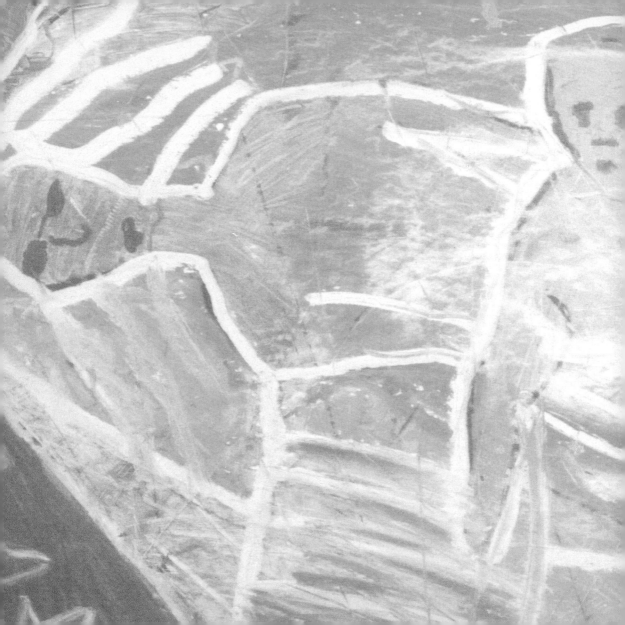

CYCLES OF CREATION

Each individual human life is part of a greater cycle of evolution; the soul journeys through successive births and deaths, learning and developing as it goes. In the same way, the soul of mankind as a whole is on a journey, and takes on different forms of which our present *homo sapiens* is just one manifestation. On a greater scale still are the world cycles in which whole universes may come into being and pass away.

THE THREE GREAT LAWS OF CREATION

Beyond the turning wheel of creation lie the three great divine laws, recognized in many mystical traditions (as the Trinity, or the Three Pillars of Kabbalah, for instance), and defined in Theosophy as:

1 **The eternal, immeasurable and unchanging principle,** which cannot be encompassed by thought or word.

2 **The eternity of the universe,** the ground for the arising of creation, and from which the shifting play of the myriad individual universes come into being.

3 **The universal oversoul,** of which every individual soul is a part.

Previous page: Interpenetrating realities within the individual, and between individuals. As in Theosophy, the vision of the artist cuts through opaque, visible reality to reveal the interconnection of life forms. Painting by Daniel Koubel.

Opposite: Just as each individual has a "root" source of energy in the body, so the human race is said by Theosophy to have "root ancestors" whose lives long ago created the foundations for our own. *The Root Chakra*, from C.W. Leadbeater.

THE CYCLES OF MANKIND

Studies of the history of mankind can pinpoint with reasonable accuracy when early Stone Age man first emerged. But they take no account of ancient myths and traditions which speak of lost races of humanity, and vanished eras of civilization. In Theosophy, these are considered to point towards past incarnations of humanity. These are known as "root races," of which our current human incarnation is said to be the fifth.

The first root race appeared just after the birth of the planet itself, but its beings did not have full physical existence. They are known as the "Moon Ancestors," because their energy comes from a long-past phase of the moon's evolution. The second is called the "Hyperborean," and its members are said to have had a kind of watery body which could shift its shape with ease. They dwelt in the northern regions of the Earth, at a time when the climate was considerably kinder than it is now! These first two root races reproduced themselves by dividing, like amoebas.

The third root race was the "Lemurian," and the first to be in full physical incarnation with sexual reproduction. The Lemurians made their home on a continent, now lost, in the area of the South Pacific and Indian oceans. Their social organization somewhat resembled ours, in that they had kings and could build a crude type of city. They worshipped a supreme deity, and at this time, it is said, an order of initiates was founded by higher beings who chose to assume bodily form and create an elect band of the wise. As the race declined (an inevitable part of the cycle) some of these initiates retreated to a place called Shambhala in the Gobi desert.

The fourth root race, the inhabitants of Atlantis, governed a great empire which was destroyed by a disastrous flood. Some Theosophists place this event at about one million years ago, and say that the most holy members of the race were saved on a few small islands and were able to pass on their teachings to our own ancestors. The last of these islands, Poseidonis, sank about 11,000 years ago.

Opposite: Here the watery, moonlit world echoes the elemental qualities of the first root races of theosophical teaching. *Keelmen Heaving in Coals by Moonlight,* by J.M.W. Turner, *c.*1835.

Now comes the fifth race, the Aryan, our own. This is the race that is developing skill in the material world, with all the opportunities for both knowledge and delusion that this implies. Since the last race, the Atlantean, perished by water, it is thought that it may be our destiny to perish by fire at the end of our run in the cycle.

Theosophists are at pains to point out that the term "race" is in no way derogatory, and that the theory of root races has nothing to do with the current use of the term to describe the different types of people in the world today. For those who find the root race theory hard to accept literally, it may be more useful to see these descriptions as representing layers of human consciousness in the rich "archeology" of the psyche.

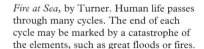

Fire at Sea, by Turner. Human life passes through many cycles. The end of each cycle may be marked by a catastrophe of the elements, such as great floods or fires.

HUMAN DESTINY

REINCARNATION

In Theosophy, the idea of reincarnation plays a strong part, aligning it with Buddhist and Hindu philosophy and opposing the conventional teachings of Christianity. Man and woman are not born into this life to be extinguished again without trace, nor are they condemned to eternal agony in hell. Hell and heaven are recognized only as transient states through which each soul must pass on that long cycle of reincarnation, as it moves from physical to immaterial states and back again on the slow and undulating wave of its journey.

The individual soul can be compared to a silver spark emerging from the divine essence. It travels on a pilgrimage in which many states of existence can be experienced, many lessons learned. Gradually, certain lessons no longer need to be repeated and the soul progresses towards its final state, union with Unity itself. Sometimes such enlightened souls do, however, choose to return to birth and to help others find the way.

An individual's progress is aided by contact with schools of wisdom; suffering on this Earth can be at least partially ameliorated by understanding of the laws of cause and effect. When we know that what we experience in this life is only a temporary and transient part of a much greater life, we need no longer feel so imprisoned and helpless. Theosophists say that we are all a part of the great body of humanity, and whatever the form of our current

Previous page: The Path, by Reginald Machell. Theosophy encourages us to embark upon our spiritual journey, and so discover the greater life of the cosmos.

Opposite: Cornfield with Crows, by Vincent van Gogh, 1890. Death and rebirth are part of the long journey of the soul. Here, the images of ripeness ready for reaping and the black crows sweeping across the cornfield are a poignant foreshadowing of the artist's own death later in the year.

incarnation—as a man or woman, black or white, poor or rich, healthy or weak—it is always a valuable learning opportunity. During the long pilgrimage, we have changed sex and status countless times.

KARMA

The principle of Necessity governs the cycle of birth and death, and is revealed in the process known as the law of karma. Karma can be related to the Christian maxim: "As ye sow, so shall ye reap." Every action has a consequence, and we cannot escape those consequences; we must shoulder them either in this world or the next, this lifetime or the next one. This is not the same as determinism, because we still face fresh choices and challenges. The pilgrim may have no control over the weather, the lie of the land, the environment he or she passes through. But there may be a choice as to where to linger, what to pass by, and where to help a fellow pilgrim.

The possibility is there to help ourselves and others. We are capable of unselfish love even without the benefits of education or a happy situation, and if we can show that love, it will automatically help those who are suffering, and perhaps influence their progress. Thus the possibility of coming closer to the divine is never denied us; it is not the exclusive privilege of initiates. Theosophy has thus always laid great emphasis on the cultivation of ethical behavior and service to society. One of its well-known leaders, Annie Besant, was also an active campaigner for English factory welfare and worked towards a better political system in India.

Opposite: Annie Besant. Originally a campaigner for free thought and population control in England, she joined the Theosophical Society in 1889 and was President of the Society from 1907 to 1933. She also founded the Central Hindu College at Benares, organized the India Home Rule League and was President of the Indian National Congress.

TIMESCALES

Interesting ideas have been discussed in Theosophy about the length of time that may occur between incarnations—taken from the human point of view, at least, for time as we know it is different on other planes of existence. The general conclusion is that the more advanced the soul, the longer it spends in between incarnations, perhaps passing only one twentieth of its time on Earth, because it does not "need" to spend so much time in an earthly form. Less developed souls, on the other hand, such as those of criminals, may be reborn almost immediately.

29

THE HIDDEN MASTERS

Master Kuthumi Lal Singh, depicted by David Aurias.

Previous page: The shifting nature of reality, captured in a photo-montage by Marko Modic.

Opposite: Monks in the mountain fastness of Ladakh, northern India.

I s any of you so eager for knowledge … as to be ready to leave your world and come into ours? Then let him come; but he must not think to return until the seal of the mysteries has locked his lips…." (Letter to A. P. Sinnett from a Master, 1880).

No aspect of Theosophy has raised such a storm of excitement as that concerning the Masters of Wisdom. Arguments have raged as to their true nature and form. Are they real adepts, long-lived, with the power to project their images when they choose? Do they live in a remote citadel in Tibet, guiding human destiny? Are they the inner force of conscience prompting us to embrace love and compassion? Or are they a level of Mind which speaks to us through whatever kind of projections we can most easily perceive?

The general view within Theosophy, shorn of its extremes, could be summarized thus: There are beings, human or once human, who have transcended the normal frontiers of knowledge, and who make their wisdom available to others. These are known as the Masters, or Mahatmas. Their teachings do not necessarily take place on the physical plane, but can reach us through inner channels. Each individual Master is only one manifestation of a plane of consciousness from which guidance comes to help us in our lives on Earth, and to help us learn more about the eternal truths of the universe. Together the Masters form what is known in theosophical terms as the Great White Lodge or Brotherhood.

In Buddhism, the mandala is a map or diagram of the perfected conscious mind. In all traditions meditation on archetypal forms has been used to reconstruct thought patterns, to integrate thoughts and feelings, and to free the adept from the apparent disorder of life.

Taken in this way, there is little quarrel between Theosophy and many other traditions, which acknowledge that spiritual help may come from beings on a higher plane than ourselves. Christianity has its communion of saints, Kabbalah its great lines of teaching, the philosophy of Gurdjieff its "inner circle of conscious humanity," Buddhism its Eight Great Disciples, alchemy its initiatory visions, and so on. Most traditions of wisdom fill in the "gap" between us and God, and propose ever more refined, subtle and transcendent levels of being between the physical and the divine.

EARLY REVELATIONS OF THE MASTERS

The sparks fly, however, when claims are made for exotic secret habitations for the Masters, the appearance of long-dead initiates in modern city streets, and the miraculous manifestation of their written teachings. One of the most famous examples of the latter occurred in the 1880s, when Madame Blavatsky was visiting two of her followers in India—a newspaper editor, A. P. Sinnett, and his wife. Extraordinary things began to happen, and soon psychic events took a tangible form as Mrs. Sinnett found a note from Master Kuthumi in a tree, and another under her pillow. An extra cup and saucer materialized beneath a bush at a picnic for an unexpected guest, and a missing brooch appeared in front of its owner at supper. Gradually, the focus shifted to Mr. Sinnett, who

C.W. Leadbeater, a formative influence in Theosophy, was an ordained priest. Though he forsook the confines of orthodox religion, he brought new insights from his theosophical studies into the nature of the Christian mass.

Opposite: Colonel H.S. Olcott. A veteran of the American Civil War, Olcott was the first President of the Theosophical Society.

found himself the recipient of a stream of letters apparently penned by disembodied Masters. These were eventually published as *The Mahatma Letters*, and the modern reader of these letters may feel that a rather excessive amount of their content is concerned, in a very mundane way, with the internal politics of the newly-fledged Theosophical Society.

A kind of iconography developed around the Masters, who were said to be visible on the inner plane and sometimes in physical form too. Their appearance was usually "impressive, noble, dignified, holy and serene." They had names, faces, nationalities: bearded Morya and Kuthumi , of Indian origin, Tuitit and Serapis Bey of the Egyptian Brotherhood, and a French aristocrat known as the Comte de Saint Germain.

Today's seekers may complain of a male monopoly of wisdom; modern Theosophy answers that the adepts have control over how they manifest, and will often choose the predominant form of the period. However, in theosophical terms, this is not an issue of great importance: in the cycle of evolution there is no ultimate distinction between male and female. We have all been, and will be, both.

Stories circulated that the Mahatmas were living in an inaccessible Asian location, where they formed a kind of Inner World Government. C. W. Leadbeater, a leading early Theosophist and gifted and sensitive writer on psychic matters, was nevertheless prone to technicolored visions which make fascinating reading but which few Theosophists today would take literally. Three of the Masters, he claimed, were definitely residing in Tibet in a hidden ravine. Here, where icy streams splashed, Madame Blavatsky herself had come for instruction and bathed for bodily refreshment in a rocky pool. Under one cliff lay a vast area of subterranean halls, which included an occult museum guarded by the Master Kuthumi himself. His own residence was a delightful house in the vicinity where he played the organ for recreation, and supped curry from a golden spoon.

Leadbeater claims to have had at least three real life encounters with Masters, which included a chance meeting with the Comte de Saint Germain strolling down a street in Rome, and witnessing Master Kuthumi suddenly materialize in the act of stepping over a balcony. He was not alone, for Colonel Olcott, another of Blavatsky's faithful supporters, claimed to have had a visit in his apartment from a Master who materialized flowers and rain showers there. People became very eager to see such wonders for themselves, and in a later phase of her work, H.P.B. began to rue the sensational response that the Masters had caused. In her *Key to Theosophy* she verified

Jiddu Krishnamurti was chosen when a boy in India by Annie Besant and C.W. Leadbeater to become a new World Teacher. Later, however, he turned his back on Theosophy, preferring to follow his own path—and was considered by many to be a great teacher in his own right.

that her own instruction had come from Initiates, but refused to give an ultimate ruling on who or what they were. She wrote that she regretted the way in which other individuals and societies were now claiming the authority of a Master. As far as Theosophists were concerned, she remarked tartly, the Masters were not omnipotent overlords: they neither controlled the Theosophical Society nor provided money for it.

One recent study of H.P.B.'s life concludes that the Masters she identifies were in fact real men whom she met during her travels. The Mahatma "Serapis Bey," for instance, is equated with a Coptic magician called Paolos Metamon who instructed her in Cairo. Other investigations have given the sceptic plenty of evidence to suggest that the Mahatma letters were forgeries, but the extent to which they were inspired from the realm of the Masters or crafted by human hand alone remains open to question.

THE HIERARCHY OF THE MASTERS

Theosophy has assimilated and ordered the teachings concerning the Masters over the last hundred years or so, playing down much of the early sensationalism. The Inner Teachers are often grouped hierarchically, with the highest being a semi-divine entity known as the Solar Logos, ruler of our solar system. The "Sun-Fathers" or "Sons of Mind" come next, and below them the Masters as already described. The great world teachers, such as Buddha, Christ and Krishna, are sometimes said to be among the ranks of the Masters, sometimes as spiritual energies of a higher level—the difference may depend upon whether the historical or the archetypal form of the teacher is referred to. Masters are themselves subject to the great cosmic laws of evolution, and will learn and evolve just as we do.

A further development of the schema includes the Masters of the Seven Rays, governors of seven key aspects of human life, described in one account as the Ray of Devotion, the Ray of Religion, the Ray of Action, the Ray of Trade, the Ray of Healing, the Ray of Art, and the Ray of Knowledge. This is sometimes seen as a more localized concentration of the Masters, a kind of subgroup with a special brief for human affairs, and it is said that the feeling of being creatively inspired in our work may come from these inner contacts.

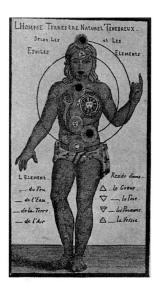

The seventeenth-century German mystic Johann Gichtel linked terrestrial man with the stars and elements in a system which corresponds to the chakras of Hindu and Buddhist thought. These represent a hierarchy of psychic centers in the body which, when energized, generate psychic states or moods within the individual.

BECOMING A PUPIL

Becoming a *chela* is a matter of treading the path to the point where one is ready for an inner contact with the Master. Theosophy does not contain any formal ceremony of initiation for this, maintaining that one's own readiness is the trigger. Sometimes, it is thought, even a comparatively advanced student may still have to wait for inner instruction if he or she has certain lessons of karma to learn first. The Masters cannot overlook a potential pupil, because they have a constant overview of all souls in the world, and one that is ready for chelaship will stand out from the rest like "the flame of a lighthouse."

MYTH OR FACT?

We can become over-obsessed with the question as to whether something "really" happened. A myth can be "true," without being historically accurate. Meaning and the mystic experience are not tied to a literal interpretation of events. Quarrels about the "authenticity" of the Mahatmas are ultimately of less interest than the proposal that we can have access to a level of higher consciousness and knowledge. Different traditions may describe the forms of this level in varying ways, because the way in which we perceive the play of divine energy in this realm may depend at least in part upon our conditioning and our training.

A three-dimensional representation of the seven levels of spiritual evolution, with a "cross section" for easier identification. From outer to inner, they are defined here as: Oneness; Causal Level; Subtle Plane; Psychic Heart; Psychology and Thought; Biology; Physical Matter.

Whether Blavatsky manipulated events to establish the identity of the Theosophical Masters, and pushed matters too far, is open to debate. Other schools in recent centuries have also woven myths around their source: the Rosicrucians and the Order of the Golden Dawn both kick-started their organizations by circulating stories of semi-miraculous events. A myth is a way of setting up a dialog between visible and invisible worlds, and, it could be said, arises out of mutual creative play between the divine and the human.

Krishnamurti with Annie Besant at the Theosophical Society headquarters in Adyar, near Madras.

SUBTLE BODIES

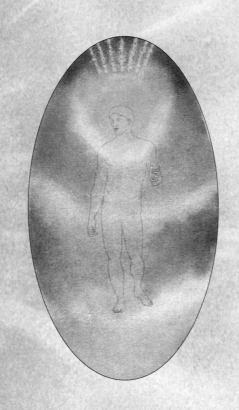

By
W. B. CROW
D.Sc., Ph.D.

THE SCIENCE
OF DREAMS

Just as our lives do not stop at death, so our bodies are not limited by their outer physical form. We exist on a number of different levels at once, from the most physical to the most spiritual. Indeed in one sense there is no difference between physical and spiritual, only the gradations that lie between the two ends of the spectrum. And, as people may divide up the spectrum of color in slightly different ways, so there are variations in the way that different Theosophists name and describe the "subtle bodies."

SEVEN SUBTLE BODIES

The general theosophical view is that we have seven subtle bodies, four of which relate to our personal existence in this particular incarnation, and three of which are supra-personal. Blavatsky called these three the "imperishable triad;" they correspond to the Three Great Laws of Creation, which we met in Chapter Two. Man is a microcosm of the greater creation, and so we should expect to find a reflection of the universal pattern within the individual human life. The three highest planes (in descending order) are given Sanskrit names and described as:

7   *Atma:* Life as a pure radiation of the Absolute.
6   *Buddhi:* the vehicle of the universal spirit.
5   *Manas:* the realm of cause and effect, where the key to the future karmic destiny of the soul is held.

Below these come the intuitive, mental, astral and physical bodies of the individual. These have their own kinds of energy and their own powers too: in the astral body, for instance, we not only have the ability to feel emotionally, but to project those emotions far beyond their specific source.

The physical body, the last link in the chain, has what is known as an etheric double, a kind of vital image of the body itself. The two are said to be connected by a silver cord, which is snapped at death. People who "leave the body" (experiences of hovering above the body are very common) may be traveling in this displaced etheric body, and those frustrating semi-dreams in which you think you are waking up and moving around, may also be an activation of the etheric double.

Moving upwards through the levels, we come next to the astral body, where our desires and feelings reside. After death, the etheric body soon dissolves and the astral body takes over. Death, in theosophical terms, is a process of shedding these different "sheaths," and moving through the seven worlds to the highest

Page 43: A painting of the mental body of Developed Man, from C.W. Leadbeater.

Opposite: The world of dreams offers us an opportunity to leave everyday reality; in dreams we may often operate in our "astral" body—hence the common experience of flying. Frontispiece of *The Science of Dreams,* by W.B. Crow.

point of which the soul is capable, before it descends again in rebirth. Each of the subtle bodies may be experienced very fully after death. On the astral plane, the soul must experience every unfulfilled desire and every unappeased emotion: this, say the Theosophists, is the real meaning of purgatory or hell.

The mental and intuitional bodies are also known as the devachanic realms. Normally, our powers of thought and cognition are filtered through the astral and physical bodies, and their effects are thus limited by these, but they can be cultivated, so that we can experience them more fully. These bodies can also be called our "higher senses," and the experience of them is said to be blissful. There is a crystal clarity, the ability to scan a wide horizon of knowledge, to put the question and know the answer in the same instant.

EXPERIMENTING WITH THE INNER PLANES

Events can resonate on more than one level. C. W. Leadbeater reports an experiment where "thought messages" were sent to absent friends. One investigator observed the effect on the mental plane, and saw the transmissions as a kind of "vibrating shell," spreading out like ripples in a pool. Another investigator surveyed the astral plane and noted that an image or color would form there, and might be seen as a kind of envoy, such as a "beautiful

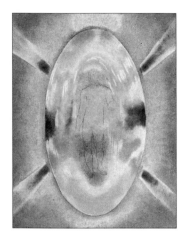

The aura of Developed Man—a harmonious balance of colors without undue muddiness usually typifies a more advanced and purified state of being.

Opposite: The science of reading the aura has been developed to a high degree by theosophists, and in this system each color that may be "seen" by the psychic can be defined as a particular thought or emotion. Leadbeater's key to the meaning of colors.

flashing golden-yellow messenger." The person for whom the message was intended would not necessarily notice anything straight away, but might be receptive only during a suitable gap in the normal hustle and bustle of daily life. This is one reason why we may receive premonitions and intuitions in dreams, when the usual activity ceases.

THE AURA

To a sensitive eye, the subtle bodies take visible form in the "aura" (a Greek word, meaning breeze). The aura is generally perceived as an egg-shaped halo around the whole person, and is composed of emanations from all the subtle bodies, which are often seen as colors. The trained "reader" of the aura may be able to gather information about the person's physical and emotional well-being from these color-energies, and there are specific bodies of teachings, not only in Theosophy, about their interpretation.

1 High spirituality	1 Devotion mixed with Affection	1 Devotion to a Noble Ideal	1 Pure Religious Feeling	1 Selfish Religous Feeling
2 Religious Feeling tinged with fear	2 Highest Intellect	2 Strong Intellect	2 Low type of Intellect	2 Pride
3 Sympathy	3 Love for Humanity	3 Unselfish Affection	3 Selfish Affection	3 Pure Affection
4 Adaptability	4 Jealousy	4 Deceit	4 Fear	4 Depression
5 Selfishness	5 Avarice	5 Anger	5 Sensuality	5 Malice

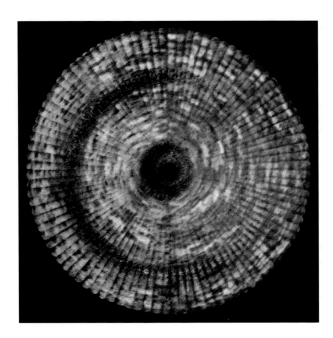

The chakras, energy centers of the body, can be perceived as dynamic wheels of color. *The Brow Chakra,* from Leadbeater.

COLOR ENERGY

Theosophical research into subtle bodies, colors and auras was greatly furthered by the work of C. W. Leadbeater and Annie Besant, who are sometimes known as the "second generation Theosophists." Annie Besant, born in 1847, was a passionate Irishwoman who left an unhappy marriage to a clergyman, studied science and medicine at university, and became president of the Theosophical Society in 1907. Her writings show a particular interest in the interpretation of color. She argued that devotional thought is perceived as pure blue, while brutal anger is a lurid dull red, and a more noble rage a vivid scarlet. Affection reveals itself through rosy hues, and intellectual activity through the yellow area of the spectrum. In general, the more wholesome the emotion, the clearer the hue, while selfish, ugly feelings tend to be muddy in color.

THOUGHT-FORMS

Our thoughts also create "thought-forms," which are not necessarily separate from our emotions, and can in fact be the impulses from which emotional responses grow. The astral coloring of emotional energy may be matched by a vibration which takes a specific form in the mental body. Thus, Theosophists warn us to train ourselves towards helpful and wholesome thought-impulses and feelings as even that which is outwardly unexpressed will have its effect. The words that we use carry their own charge, and it has been argued that unnecessary, casual use of words like "hate" always stir up their emotional astral associations. Forms of wording used in ceremonies or ritual will also "resonate" through the inner planes, and thus should always be chosen with great care.

Thought-forms of two mourners at a funeral. On the right is the despair, fear and selfishness of the man who cannot see beyond the fact of physical death. On the left is the clarity, compassion and devotion of the enlightened man. These demonstrate how knowledge of the truth takes away all fear of death. From A. Besant and C.W. Leadbeater.

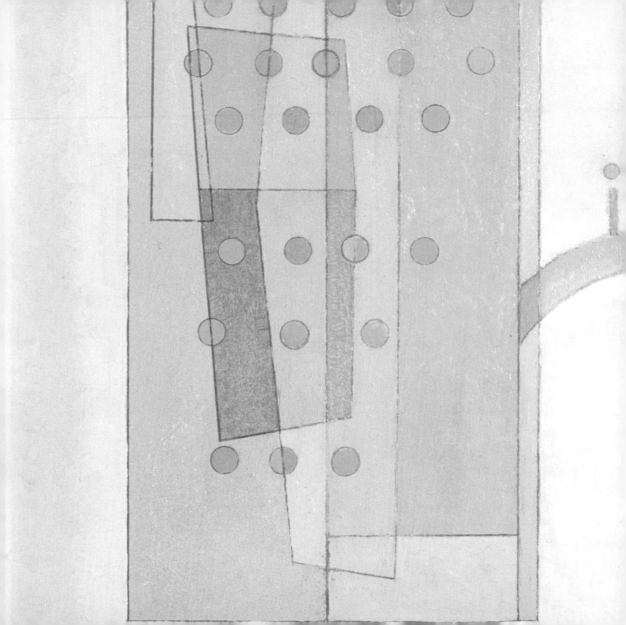

THEOSOPHY TODAY

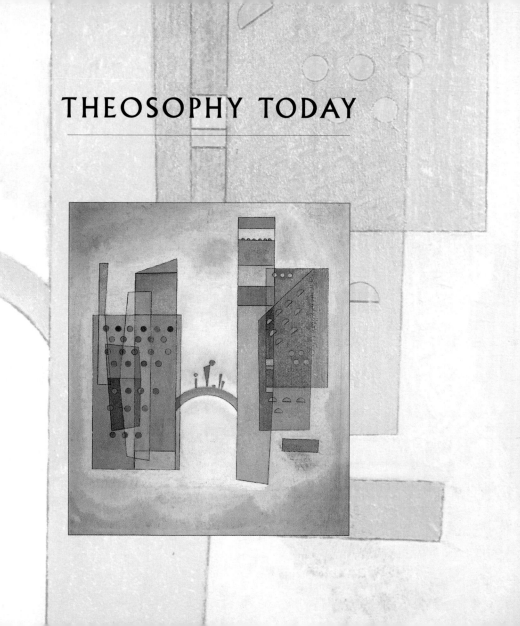

THERE IS NO RELIGION HIGHER THAN TRUTH

After a brief walk along the theosophical path, we can see that there are different ways of looking at the term Theosophy. In its root form, meaning those who search for Divine Wisdom, it is perennial, and cannot be restricted to any one religion or culture. In the specific form we have been using, it applies to the body of teachings which have arisen out of the efforts of Madame Blavatsky and her followers to synthesize something of that wisdom from a range of great teachings and traditions. The work of the Theosophist is to grasp that wisdom, and apply it in the ethics of everyday living. And, in a third respect, it is closely associated with the organization called the Theosophical Society, which remains the main vehicle for transmitting these teachings today.

This distinction is made because it is worth remembering that whereas wisdom is eternal, human interpretations of that wisdom are always colored by time and place. They are a means to work towards that universality, not the literal manifestation of it. Madame Blavatsky herself warned against becoming too attached to any one particular image or vision, for it will inevitably be replaced by a new one as true growth takes place.

Previous page: The Bridge, by Wassily Kandinsky (1866–1944), one of several turn-of-the-century artists whose work was profoundly influenced by contact with Theosophy. The bridge can be perceived as symbolizing the crossing of the abyss to a new world.

Opposite: An abstract vision of the wheel of life, by Daniel Koubel.

THE ACHIEVEMENTS OF THEOSOPHY

Theosophy has already achieved a great deal in bringing the teachings of Buddhism and Indian philosophy to the West, and of opening the European mind to the idea that no one religion or system has a monopoly of the truth. It has brought material from different traditions to our attention, including aspects of our own culture such as alchemy and Neo-Platonism, and has helped to create a sense of the relationship between all great world teachings. The debt to Theosophy has recently been acknowledged thus in a survey of Western esotericism: "Together with the Western occult tradition, the Theosophists have provided almost all the underpinnings of the "New Age" movement."

How Theosophy will evolve through the coming generations waits to be seen; there is plenty of relevant "source material" and theosophical writings which can be drawn out and worked on; for example, the concise description of psychic phenomena and subtle bodies in the works of C. W. Leadbeater and Annie Besant has probably never been bettered, and could be studied to great effect in the context of modern therapies and personal development programs.

Opposite: Mandala painted by one of Jung's patients during therapy. Jung found that these ancient and universal images acted as a liberating and integrating force in the psyche.

Teachings for Today's World

Animal welfare is an area in which Theosophy has always been ahead of its time. Long before the current interest in vegetarianism and protests against intensive farming practices, Theosophists were advocating abstinence from eating meat, and the better treatment of animals. For a start, it is said that eating meat can create a "blood haze" in the aura, which makes it especially difficult to develop a living contact with the Masters. It is also said that the animals we eat usually die in terror, and that we take this in along with their meat, to our detriment.

Animals, in theosophical teaching, do have a soul, which is another reason why they should be treated with respect and compassion. But they do not have individualized souls like humans, which continue as entities after death. Each animal soul is, as it were, water scooped out from the "group soul" of that species, and at death the water returns to the pool. Only rarely when an animal has reached a certain level of development can it cross that abyss and become individualized, and perhaps reborn as a human. Other theosophical teachings, once thought to be on the fringes of acceptability, have now become of great interest in the modern world. Theosophy helped to re-awaken Western interest in theories of reincarnation, for example, which are now highly topical as many people try to discover personal memories of "past lives." And teachings about the Masters link with what is now called

"channelling," teachings given directly by disembodied, spiritual entities. Attitudes in both these areas range from the fanciful to the seriously academic, but it is as though we are now at last collectively ready to face the possibility that the world of Mind is greater than the physical brain.

As above, so below. Scottish landscape photographed by Marko Modic.

Emblem of the Theosophical
Order of Service, an independent
organization dedicated to the
practical relief of suffering.

THE THEOSOPHICAL SOCIETY

The Theosophical Society today has many branches international-
ly, and is particularly strong in the United States, Australia and
New Zealand, in Britain and, of course, in India where its headquarters are situated. Local branches are known as "lodges," and
here members can meet for study in groups or for personal
research in libraries. The Society is sometimes described as a
"self-help" organization—facilities are provided, but it is up to
each individual member to work towards a real understanding of
Theosophy. This accords with the more individual, self-motivated
approach of today; Theosophy has always insisted that members
should respect each other's beliefs, and a member can only be
expelled for disobeying this rule. The principle of universal brotherhood irrespective of race or creed, which Theosophy affirms, is
more relevant than ever in today's world of nationalistic wars and
religious sectarianism.

Branches of the Theosophical Society often play host to visiting
teachers who lead classes in disciplines such as yoga, meditation,
astrology, or Tai Chi, and some teachers may themselves be
Theosophists who have taken training in other fields. Although
Theosophy does not offer its own ritual or ceremony, the potential
value of a religious structure and devotional ritual is recognized,
and many members also belong to Co-Masonry (Freemasonry for
both men and women) or the Liberal Catholic Church.

Eastern forms of meditation are widely practised today in different religions and personal development groups.

Theosophy is one of the newest shoots in the Western wisdom tradition, and is continuing to evolve. As we are still close to the point of its arising, it is not yet clear what form it will take in the future. It is possible that it will gradually become absorbed into the pan-religious approach of the New Age. More likely it will continue to carry forward a very specific body of teachings, which will be sifted, tried, and tested in the fire of time. Theosophy has already given a great deal to the Western world; now, perhaps, the work of implementing its teaching really begins.

BIBLIOGRAPHY

Useful Introductions to Theosophy

Ellwood, Robert. *Theosophy: A Modern Expression of the Wisdom of the Ages.* Wheaton, IL: Quest, 1986.

Cooper, Irving S. *Theosophy Simplified.* First published 1915; reissued Wheaton, IL: Quest, 1989.

Classic Theosophical Texts

Blavatsky, H. P. *Isis Unveiled.* First published 1877.

—— . *The Secret Doctrine.* First published 1888.

—— . *The Key to Theosophy.* First published 1889.

(Facsimile editions of these texts are available from the Theosophical University Press, Pasadena, CA.)

Life of Blavatsky

Cranston, Sylvia. *H.P.B.: The Extraordinary Life and Influence of Helena Blavatsky.* New York: Tarcher/Putnam, 1993.

Wachtmeister, Countess Constance. *Reminiscences of H. P. Blavatsky.* Wheaton, IL: Quest, 1976.

"By some of her Pupils." *In Memory of Helena Petrovna Blavatsky.* First published 1891; Centenary Edition. London: Theosophical Publishing House, 1991.

The Masters

Leadbeater, C. W. *The Masters and the Path.* Madras, India: Theosophical Publishing House, 1925.

Barker, A. T. (compiled). *The Mahatma Letters.* New York: Frederick Stokes Co., 1923.

Inner Planes
Leadbeater, C. W. *The Devachanic Plane*. First published 1896; reprinted Madras, India: Theosophical Publishing House, 1984.
Leadbeater, C. W. *The Inner Life*. First published 1912; reprinted Wheaton IL: Theosophical Publishing House, 1976, 1992.
Tansley, David V. *Subtle Body*. London: Thames and Hudson, 1977.

Modern Studies of Theosophy in Context
Godwin, Joscelyn. *The Theosophical Enlightenment*. Albany, NY: State University of New York Press, 1994.
Johnson, Paul. *The Masters Revealed*. Albany, NY: State University of New York Press, 1994.

ACKNOWLEDGMENTS

Ahmuno: 33, 34.
AKG London: 5, 12, 20, 23, 27, 51.
C.M. Dixon Photo Library: 2.
Daniel Koubel: 17, 53.
Marko Modic: 31, 57.
Sidd Murray-Clark: 10.
Premgit: 59.
Theosophical Society in England: 3, 7, 8, 9, 13, 15, 29, 37, 38, 41, 52.
Theosophical Publishing House, Adyar: iv, 1, 11, 19, 36, 39, 42, 43, 44, 46, 47, 48, 49.
Theosophical University Press, Pasedena, CA: 25.
Yatri: 40.